MW01139331

THE LIFE OF
JOSEPH BRANT

WILL ROGERS LIBRARY
1515 N. FLORENCE
CLAREMORE, OK 74017

RYAN NAGELHOUT

New York

Published in 2017 by The Rosen Publishing Group, Inc.
29 East 21st Street, New York, NY 10010

Copyright © 2017 by The Rosen Publishing Group, Inc.

All rights reserved. No part of this book may be reproduced in any form without permission in writing from the publisher, except by a reviewer.

First Edition

Editor: Sarah Machajewski
Book Design: Katelyn Heinle/Tanya Dellaccio

Photo Credits: Cover Stock Montage/Archive Photos/Getty Images; cover (background) Michael Shake/Shutterstock.com; p. 5 George Romney/Getty Images; p. 7 https://en.wikipedia.org/wiki/Sir_William_Johnson,_1st_Baronet#/media/File:Sir_William_Johnson.png; p. 9 Raymond B. Summers/Shutterstock.com; p. 11 https://upload.wikimedia.org/wikipedia/commons/3/32/Johnson_saving_Dieskau.jpg; p. 13 Interim Archives/Getty Images; p. 15 Danita Delimont/Gallo Images/Getty Images; p. 17 https://en.wikipedia.org/wiki/Joseph_Brant#/media/File:Joseph_Brant_by_Gilbert_Stuart_1786_oil_on_canvas jpeg; p. 19 https://en.wikipedia.org/wiki/United_States_Declaration_of_Independence#/media/File:United_States_Declaration_of_Independence.jpg; p. 21 (left) https://en.wikipedia.org/wiki/Red_Jacket#/media/File:Red_Jacket_2.jpg; p. 21 (right) https://en.wikipedia.org/wiki/Cornplanter#/media/File:Cornplanter.jpg; p. 23 Hulton Archive/Archive Photos/Getty Images; p. 24 https://en.wikipedia.org/wiki/Treaty_of_Paris_(1783)#/media/File:Treaty_of_Paris_1783_-_last_page_(hi-res).jpg; p. 25 https://upload.wikimedia.org/wikipedia/commons/b/b8/Surrender_of_Lord_Cornwallis.jpg; p. 27 meunierd/Shutterstock.com; p. 29 Toronto Star Archives/Getty Images.

Library of Congress Cataloging-in-Publication Data

Nagelhout, Ryan, author.
 The life of Joseph Brant / Ryan Nagelhout
     pages cm. — (Native American biographies)
 Includes index.
 ISBN 978-1-5081-4823-4 (pbk.)
 ISBN 978-1-5081-4782-4 (6 pack)
 ISBN 978-1-5081-4817-3 (library binding)
 1. Brant, Joseph, 1742-1807—Juvenile literature. 2. Mohawk Indians—Biography—Juvenile literature. 3. Indians of North America—Wars—1750-1815—Juvenile literature. I. Title.
 E99.M8N33 2016
 974.7004'9755420092—dc23
 [B]
                              2015032596

Manufactured in the United States of America

CPSIA Compliance Information: Batch #BS16PK: For Further Information contact Rosen Publishing, New York, New York at 1-800-237-9932

CONTENTS

TWO SIDES OF HISTORY

Joseph Brant was a Mohawk military officer who fought courageously for his people. He was also a translator, a peacekeeper, and a religious **missionary**. His 65 years brought him many different kinds of fame. He was feared throughout the Mohawk Valley for his military abilities. Britain's royal court knew him for his efforts on behalf of the throne. Many Native American people came to rely on his leadership as settlers arrived on their lands.

The story of Joseph Brant is much more complicated than just "good" and "bad." His life was full of enemies and supporters, and it's easy to end up on the wrong side of history. In the case of Joseph Brant, the value of his life's work depends on whom you ask.

WHAT'S IN A NAME?

THERE ARE A FEW DIFFERENT NAMES FOR THE PEOPLE THAT OCCUPIED NORTH AMERICA BEFORE EUROPEANS ARRIVED. SETTLERS FIRST CALLED THEM "INDIANS" BECAUSE THEY MISTAKENLY THOUGHT THEY HAD SAILED AROUND THE WORLD AND LANDED IN THE EAST INDIES. IN THE MODERN UNITED STATES, THESE GROUPS OF PEOPLE ARE OFTEN REFERRED TO AS NATIVE AMERICANS OR AMERICAN INDIANS. IN CANADA, THEY ARE CALLED FIRST NATIONS OR ABORIGINAL PEOPLES.

Brant was a leader among his people, but not all native people liked and supported him.

Thayeadanegea,
Joseph Brant
the Mohawk C...

BORN ON A RIVER

Joseph Brant was born in present-day Ohio in 1742 on the banks of the Muskingum River, which is a **tributary** of the Ohio River. Brant was given the Mohawk name Thayendanegea, which means "he who places two bets" or "two sticks bound together for strength."

Joseph Brant's family history is a subject of much **debate**. His mother was a Mohawk woman. Some records show that she and her husband **converted** to Christianity and took the names Margaret and Peter Tehonwaghkwangearahkwa. Some say he was the son of an Englishman named Sir William Johnson, but this has never been proven true. Joseph's mother remarried after her first husband died. Her second husband was Brant Kanagaradunkwa. Joseph and his half-sister Molly took Brant as their last name.

Brant's family moved to the Mohawk River Valley in present-day New York after his father passed away. Brant eventually came to know white settlers in the area, including Sir William Johnson, who is pictured here.

THE IROQUOIS

THE MOHAWK PEOPLE ARE PART OF THE HAUDENOSAUNEE CULTURE. THE ENGLISH CALLED THEM THE IROQUOIS. IN EARLY COLONIAL TIMES, THE HAUDENOSAUNEE WERE FIVE GROUPS—THE SENECAS, CAYUGAS, ONONDAGAS, ONEIDAS, AND MOHAWKS—WHO SPOKE SIMILAR LANGUAGES AND LIVED AROUND PRESENT-DAY NEW YORK STATE. IN 1722, THE TUSCARORAS JOINED THE HAUDENOSAUNEE AFTER MOVING TO THE AREA FROM THE SOUTHEASTERN UNITED STATES. TOGETHER, THE GROUPS BECAME KNOWN AS THE SIX NATIONS. THE NATIONS WERE BROUGHT TOGETHER TO PROTECT THEIR INTERESTS AND MAKE DECISIONS AS A GROUP.

SIR WILLIAM JOHNSON

THE YOUNG MOHAWK

Life for Native American children in North America was very different than it is today. The Mohawk people lived a quiet life, keeping other groups of people out of their area. Few settlers came into the Mohawk Valley. Brant often played games, fished, and paddled canoes with his friends. Slowly, though, the Mohawks came into contact with traders traveling through the valley.

British settlers also slowly began moving into the Mohawks' homelands. Sir William Johnson was the **superintendent** of Indian affairs and often worked with Haudenosaunee leaders on matters between native people and settlers. Johnson was an important man to many Mohawks, but he quickly became a big part of Brant's life. Johnson often stayed at the home of Brant's stepfather. Johnson noticed Brant's half-sister, Molly, and they soon began a relationship.

One story says Johnson noticed Molly Brant at a parade when she skillfully rode a horse. He asked Molly to be his housekeeper, and she took care of his children and his household. They lived at Fort Johnson and Johnson Hall in New York, which is pictured here.

OFF TO BATTLE

Brant may have begun traveling with Sir William Johnson when he was around 13 years old. Brant was smart and a fast learner, and Johnson had been put in charge of his own military unit. The teenager was allowed to fight with Johnson in what became known as the French and Indian War.

The French and Indian War lasted from 1754 to 1763. It was fought between the British and the French over land in North America. The war began because the British were unhappy French settlers were expanding their territory in the Ohio River Valley. Many of these lands were home to native groups, which drew them into the war. Different groups fought on different sides of the conflict. Brant fought with Johnson in support of the British. Brant took part in his first battle in 1758 at Lake George.

The French and Indian War lasted nine years. Britain received land in present-day Canada from the French and Florida from Spain in the 1763 peace conference that ended the war.

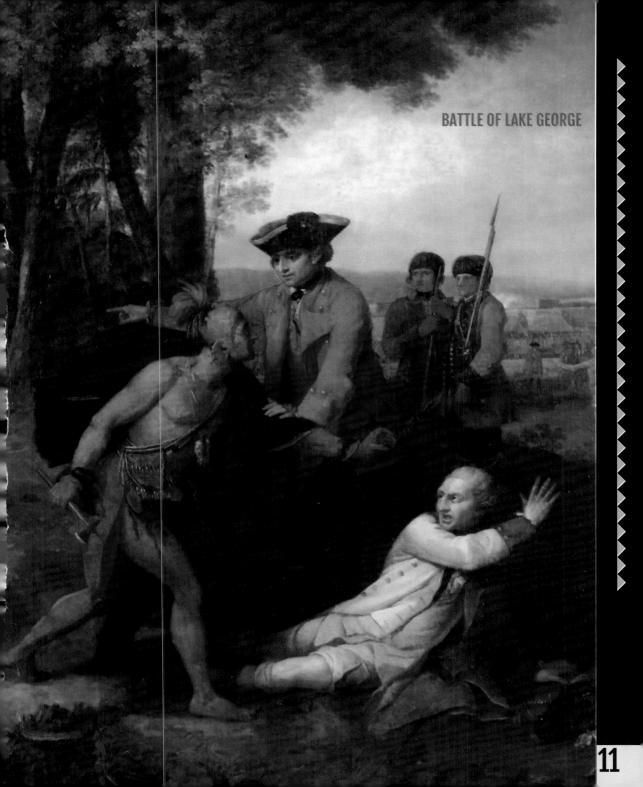

SCHOOLING AND MISSION WORK

In 1761, Brant was sent to Moor's Charity School in Lebanon, Connecticut. He learned to read and write in English and studied the Bible. While at school, he converted to the Anglican Church. Brant left school in 1763 to work as an interpreter for a Christian missionary. He also worked on translating a book in the Bible and a prayer book into the Mohawk language.

A year later, Brant left the missionary. He planned to go to a college in New York City. However, his plans were interrupted. Fighting broke out between some Native American groups and white settlers in a conflict known as Pontiac's Rebellion. This caused much hostility, or anger, toward Native Americans, and Sir William Johnson felt Brant wouldn't be safe at school.

PONTIAC'S REBELLION

IN 1763, CHIEF PONTIAC OF THE OTTOWA PEOPLE LED SEVERAL NATIVE AMERICAN GROUPS IN ATTACKS AGAINST BRITISH FORTS. PONTIAC AND OTHER LEADERS WERE UNHAPPY WITH MANY OF THE BRITISH ARMY'S POLICIES AFTER THE FRENCH AND INDIAN WAR. THEY ALSO FELT WHITE SETTLERS WERE TAKING OVER THEIR LANDS. KNOWN AS PONTIAC'S REBELLION, THE VIOLENT CONFLICT SAW THE BURNING OF MANY FORTS AND THE DEATHS OF HUNDREDS OF COLONISTS. EVENTUALLY, THE BRITISH GOVERNMENT CHANGED SOME OF THE POLICIES THAT CAUSED THE CONFLICT. PONTIAC'S REBELLION ENDED WITH THE SIGNING OF A PEACE TREATY IN 1766.

Chief Pontiac, pictured here, united many Native American groups against the British, who gained control of his people's homelands after the French and Indian War.

SETTLING DOWN

In July 1765, Brant married an Oneida woman named Margaret. The two settled in Canajoharie, which was a village along the Mohawk River near present-day Albany, New York. They lived in a house that Brant had received after his stepfather's death. Brant owned about 80 acres (32.4 ha) of farmland, and the couple raised corn and livestock. The Brants had two children, Isaac and Christiana.

As white settlers continued to move west, the Mohawk people were faced with the problem of losing more and more of their land. Settlers fought Mohawks not with weapons, but with complicated court cases called lawsuits. Many Mohawks didn't understand the language and were forced unfairly off their land. Brant acted as an interpreter for many Mohawks in these cases.

Brant and Margaret lived in Canajoharie, which is pictured here. They often welcomed Christian missionaries to stay in their home. Margaret died of tuberculosis in 1771 or 1772. Brant remarried, but his second wife also died of the disease.

TIME IN ENGLAND

Sir William Johnson died in 1774. His nephew, Guy Johnson, took over his responsibilities. Brant became Johnson's secretary and also received a captain's commission. In 1774 or 1775, Brant and Johnson traveled to Britain. Brant was presented to the royal court.

Brant impressed the British. As an educated Christian who spoke English, Brant went against the **stereotypes** they had of native people. At this time, some people felt Native Americans fit an idea known as the "noble savage." This idea teaches that Native Americans were uncivilized and simple, which made them "good" because they weren't influenced by society's evils. It spread the belief that native people were "outsiders" or "different." Today, this idea is seen as **racist**.

ROMANTIC RACISM

THE IDEA THAT NATIVES WERE "NOBLE SAVAGES" IS AN EXAMPLE OF SOMETHING CALLED ROMANTIC RACISM. SOME WHITE SETTLERS BELIEVED NATIVE AMERICANS WERE SIMPLE PEOPLE AND UNEQUAL TO EUROPEANS. SOME THOUGHT THEY WERE LESS THAN HUMAN, WHICH IS SOMETHING THEY ALSO FELT ABOUT BLACK SLAVES. IN REALITY, NATIVE TRIBES HAD **COMPLEX** SOCIAL STRUCTURES, **CUSTOMS**, AND TRADITIONS. BRANT WAS FAMILIAR WITH EUROPEANS AND THEIR WAYS, BUT KNEW THEY DIDN'T SEE HIM AS THEIR EQUAL. HE WORKED HARD TO PROVE HIMSELF TO OTHERS.

British artist Gilbert Stuart painted this portrait of Brant in 1786. The painting was sold in 2014.

AMERICAN INDEPENDENCE

While Brant and Johnson were in Britain, colonists were pushing for independence from Great Britain. British troops and colonists clashed at Lexington and Concord in Massachusetts in 1775. The colonies and British were officially at war. The next year, the American colonies adopted the Declaration of Independence.

Both the British and the colonists came to the Haudenosaunee people asking them to stay neutral, or to not pick a side in the fighting. The Native American groups were even discussed by the Continental Congress, which was the group that issued the Declaration of Independence and governed the colonies during the American Revolution. The Haudenosaunee Grand Council met at Onondaga, which is near present-day Syracuse, New York, to discuss its part in the war. The council decided it would remain neutral—but things soon changed.

The Colonies' Committee for Indian Affairs suggested that colonists "treat the Indians, who behave peaceably and inoffensively, with kindness and civility...." Later reports suggested that Native Americans were not treated this way.

DECLARATION OF INDEPENDENCE

RANT WAS IN BRITAIN, HE MET LORD GEORGE GERMAIN, WHO WAS A COLONIAL

L. BRANT USED THIS TIME TO TRY TO CONVINCE GERMAIN TO HELP THE

NOSAUNEE KEEP COLONISTS OFF NATIVE LAND. GERMAIN AGREED TO HELP THE

NOSAUNEE AND ENFORCE THE TREATY IF BRANT COULD PROMISE THEY WOULD BE

KING. BRANT WAS WILLING TO PROMISE TO HELP THE BRITISH IF IT COULD HELP H

HE SAID. "WE ARE TIRED [OF] MAKING COMPLAINTS AND GETTING NO **REDRESS**."

A LEAGUE DIVIDED

The Six Nations of the Haudenosaunee people could not agree on what action they should take during the American Revolution. This caused a division, with some nations wanting to support the British and others wanting to support the colonists. The nations met in Oswego, New York, in 1777.

Brant and the Mohawks wanted to side with the British and help their cause, while others—led by Seneca leaders Red Jacket and Cornplanter—wanted the groups to stay neutral. Brant argued that the Haudenosaunee needed to help the British, who would help keep colonists off their lands. Three nations—the Senecas, Onondagas, and Cayugas—joined the Mohawks and other Native American groups from Ohio in supporting the British. The Haudenosaunee's unity was broken, and its nations prepared for war.

THE FIRE GOES OUT

DISEASE ALSO PLAYED A PART IN DIVIDING THE HAUDENOSAUNEE. THE MEETING BETWEEN TRIBES BRANT ORGANIZED IN OSWEGO IN 1777 CAME AFTER AN **EPIDEMIC** HIT THE NATIVE POPULATION. THREE CHIEFS, CALLED SACHEMS, AND MORE THAN 80 OTHER IMPORTANT HAUDENOSAUNEE LEADERS DIED BEFORE ANOTHER GRAND COUNCIL FIRE COULD BE HELD AT ONONDAGA. WITHOUT A CENTRAL BODY TO MAKE DECISIONS, INDIVIDIAL NATIONS WERE LEFT TO MAKE THEIR OWN CHOICES ABOUT WHICH SIDE TO TAKE IN THE REVOLUTION.

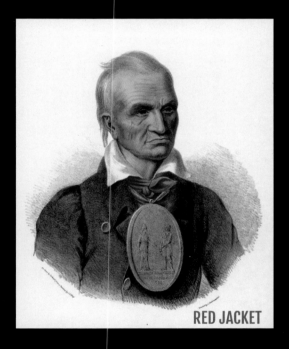

RED JACKET

CORNPLANTER

Seneca leaders Red Jacket (also known as Sagoyewatha) and Cornplanter hoped to stay neutral, but their nations eventually helped Brant fight for the British during the revolution.

RAIDING PARTIES

Brant proved to be a very good military commander, leading **raids** against colonists during the American Revolution. He skillfully led a group of Native Americans in the Battle of Oriskany on August 6, 1777. Brant also led troops of Native Americans to raid a number of forts and villages.

Colonists fought back by burning Haudenosaunee villages. In response, Brant led a raid on a well-protected village called Cherry Valley on November 11, 1778. After these attacks, Brant gained a reputation as a feared military leader.

Brant also helped the British off the battlefield. During the American Revolution, Brant stopped Chief Red Jacket's attempt to convince other Haudenosaunee nations to make peace with the colonists. Despite Brant's military successes, the British cause was struggling in other areas of the war.

This illustration is an artist's version of what may have happened during Brant's raid against Cherry Valley. In the image, a Native American man is about to attack a white man and woman, while their home is burned in the background.

AFTER THE WAR

In the fall of 1781, British general Lord Charles Cornwallis was trapped near Yorktown and the Atlantic Ocean. He surrendered on October 19, a turning point for the colonists in the Revolutionary War. The Treaty of Paris ended the American Revolution on September 3, 1783. The treaty recognized the independence of the United States and officially gave the new nation a lot of land.

Brant and the Mohawks lost the war, their villages, and their **allies** in North America. They were also in danger of completely losing their lands. Native Americans signed a number of treaties with the U.S. government over the next few years. The treaties saw Native Americans give up their land and be falsely promised that their rights would be protected. Slowly, most of the Haudenosaunee population was pushed out of what became New York State, but some remained on **reservations**.

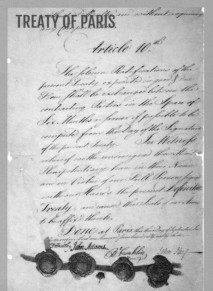

TREATY OF PARIS

The end of the American Revolution created the United States. Native groups living near the colonies, which were now states, were pressured to give up their land as more settlers moved west.

LATER IN LIFE

Despite losing the war, Britain still had claims to land in North America. This land north of the Great Lakes and the new United States later became Canada. Because Brant and the Mohawks remained faithful to the British cause during the American Revolution, Britain gave them more than 600,000 acres (242,811 ha) of land along the Grand River in present-day Ontario.

Brant moved with his people to the land given to them by the British. The Mohawks lived there peacefully, and Brant encouraged other Native American groups to work with Americans and sign peace treaties with them. Brant kept his role as captain in the British army and continued to work as a missionary. However, once the war ended, Native American groups saw their ways of life change greatly.

Brant continued his missionary work later in life, visiting England again in 1785 and raising money for a new church in Upper Canada.

FOR HIS PEOPLE

Brant died in his home in Burlington, Ontario, on November 24, 1807. Before he died, he reportedly said, "Have pity on the poor Indians. If you have any influence with the great, **endeavor** to use it for their good."

From the time he was young, Joseph Brant's life was affected by European strangers who came to his homelands to start a new life. Their new lives were made at the expense of Native Americans like Brant, who lost their home and their rights as Europeans moved in. Brant was one of the few people living in North America during that time who saw both sides of the struggles between European settlers and Native Americans. His story is an important one to remember, both as a lesson in American history and the history of the Mohawk people.

THE BRANT MUSEUM

JOSPEPH BRANT'S HOME IN BURLINGTON IS NOW A MUSEUM WHERE VISITORS CAN LEARN MORE ABOUT HIS LIFE AND THE MOHAWK PEOPLE. THE MUSEUM IS ACTUALLY A REPRODUCTION OF HIS HOME. CONSTRUCTON STARTED IN 1937 AND THE MUSEUM OPENED IN 1942. THE MUSEUM DISPLAYS PERSONAL ITEMS OWNED AND USED BY BRANT AND TELLS PEOPLE THE STORY OF ONE OF THE MORE CONTROVERSIAL CHARACTERS OF THE AMERICAN REVOLUTION.

The Brant Museum features the Joseph Brant Hallway, which is filled with paintings and other objects once owned by Brant.

TIMELINE OF JOSEPH BRANT'S LIFE

1742 Thayendanegea, later known as Joseph Brant, is born in present-day Ohio.

1750s Brant's half-sister Molly begins a relationship with Sir William Johnson.

1754–1763 The French and Indian War takes place in North America.

1761 Brant attends Moor's Charity School.

1765 Brant marries his first wife, Margaret.

1774 Brant becomes secretary for Guy Johnson.

1775 The American Revolution begins. One year later, the American colonies adopt the Declaration of Independence. The Haudenosaunee split over which side of the fighting to support.

1777 Brant leads raids on forts and commands troops in the Battle of Oriskany, where he earns a reputation for his military successes.

1778 Brant leads a raid on the village of Cherry Valley.

1783 The American Revolution ends. After the war, Brant and other Mohawks move near the Grand River near present-day Ontario.

1785 Brant travels to England to raise money for the Christian Church.

1807 Brant dies on November 24.

1942 The Joseph Brant Museum opens in Burlington, Ontario.

GLOSSARY

ally: Someone who is on your side.

complex: Having many parts.

convert: To change one's beliefs.

custom: A traditional way of doing something.

debate: An argument or question.

endeavor: To try hard to do something.

epidemic: A sickness that spreads widely and affects many people at once.

missionary: A person who works to spread their religion.

racist: Having or showing the belief that one race is better than another.

raid: A sudden attack.

redress: Something that makes up for a problem.

reservation: Land set aside by the U.S. government for a Native American group or groups to live on.

stereotype: A widely held, but usually oversimplified, belief about something or someone.

superintendent: A person who directs or manages something.

tributary: A small river that flows into a larger one.

INDEX

WEBSITES

Due to the changing nature of Internet links, PowerKids Press has developed an online list of websites related to the subject of this book. This site is updated regularly. Please use this link to access the list: www.powerkidslinks.com/natv/bran